Consultants

Ashley Bishop, Ed.D.
Sue Bishop, M.E.D.

Publishing Credits

Dona Herweck Rice, *Editor-in-Chief*
Robin Erickson, *Production Director*
Lee Aucoin, *Creative Director*
Tim J. Bradley, *Illustrator Manger*
Jason Peltz, *Illustrator*
Sharon Coan, *Project Manager*
Jamey Acosta, *Editor*
Rachelle Cracchiolo, M.A.Ed., *Publisher*

Teacher Created Materials
5301 Oceanus Drive
Huntington Beach, CA 92649-1030
http://www.tcmpub.com
ISBN 978-1-4333-2934-0
© 2012 Teacher Created Materials, Inc.
Printed in China WAI002

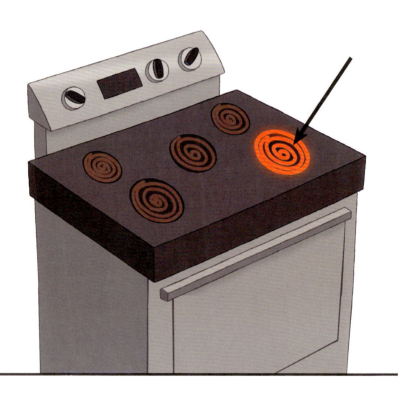

hot

Is it hot?

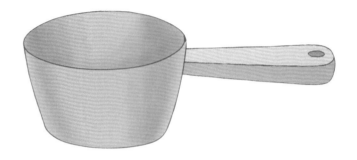

pot

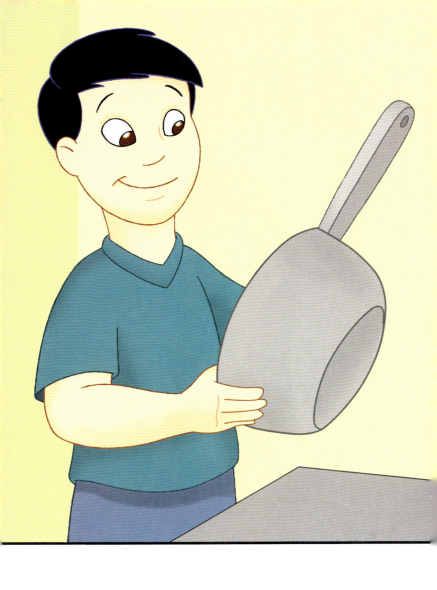

The pot is not hot.

tot

Is the tot hot?

dot

The tot has dots.

Hot!

Glossary

Sight Words

Is   it   The
not   has

Extension Activities

Read the story together with your child. Use the discussion questions before, during, and after your reading to deepen your child's understanding of the story and the rime (word family) that is introduced.

The activities provide fun ideas for continuing the conversation about the story and the vocabulary that is introduced. They will help your child make personal connections to the story and use the vocabulary to describe prior experiences.

Discussion Questions
- How do you stay safe in the kitchen?
- What kinds of things make you feel hot?
- What do we do in the kitchen to make sure that we don't get burned from something hot?

Activities at Home
- Review the story and take turns acting out the different parts. Test different kinds of expressions while you read, modeling these for your child to hear and mimic. Talk about the different ending punctuation included in the text.

- Talk about different things that can get hot in the kitchen. Choose all sorts of kitchen-related materials and appliances to discuss. Have your child respond with two different sentences: *It is not hot. It is hot.*